COURTING  HISTORY

Affirmative Action

*Regents of the University
of California v. Bakke*

ZACHARY DEIBEL

Cavendish
Square

New York

Published in 2019 by Cavendish Square Publishing, LLC
243 5th Avenue, Suite 136, New York, NY 10016

Website: cavendishsq.com

This publication represents the opinions and views of the author based on his or her personal
experience, knowledge, and research. The information in this book serves as a general guide
only. The author and publisher have used their best efforts in preparing this book and
disclaim liability rising directly or indirectly from the use and application of this book.

All websites were available and accurate when this book was sent to press.

Library of Congress Cataloging-in-Publication Data

Names: Deibel, Zachary, author.
Title: Affirmative action : Regents of the University of California v. Bakke
/ Zachary Deibel.
Description: New York : Cavendish Square, 2018. | Series: Courting history. |
Includes bibliographical references and index.
Identifiers: LCCN 2017059329 (print) | LCCN 2017060333 (ebook) |
ISBN 9781502635815 (eBook) | ISBN 9781502635808 (library bound) |
ISBN 9781502635822 (pbk.)
Subjects: LCSH: Bakke, Allan Paul--Trials, litigation, etc.--Juvenile literature. |
University of California (System). Regents--Trials, litigation, etc.--Juvenile literature. |
Discrimination in medical education--Law and legislation--United States--
Juvenile literature. | Affirmative action programs in education--Law and legislation--
United States--Juvenile literature.
Classification: LCC KF228.B34 (ebook) | LCC KF228.B34 D45 2018 (print) |
DDC 344.73/0798--dc23
LC record available at https://lccn.loc.gov/2017059329

Editorial Director: David McNamara
Editor: Chet'la Sebree
Copy Editor: Nathan Heidelberger
Associate Art Director: Amy Greenan
Designer: Amy Greenan
Production Coordinator: Karol Szymczuk
Photo Research: J8 Media

Printed in the United States of America

Contents

ONE

The Origins of Affirmative Action

The United States of America is a nation based on equality. The Declaration of Independence, a document that legally separated the thirteen colonies from England, stated that "all men are created equal." This belief in equality is one of the country's founding principles. Despite that foundation, the United States has a history of slavery that still affects the country today. Many state and federal programs have been created to right centuries of wrongdoings. These programs offer Americans of all backgrounds equal chances to succeed. Over the years, these programs have been challenged. Many of them have started national conversations about what it means to treat people "equally."

Access to education is an important factor in achieving equality. A lack of education can stand in the way of a person's opportunities for financial stability and success. Historian Thomas Sowell argues that education is "the gateway to upward mobility." In other words, education is key to success. The Supreme Court's important decision in *Brown v. Board of Education of Topeka* ended segregation, or the legal separation of groups based on race, in state-run schools. Before the decision, segregation was a legal way to continue

The Freedmen's Bureau built schools like this one to provide education opportunities for former slaves.

to oppress African Americans after slavery. Segregated schools for African Americans were usually underfunded, and students did not receive the same level of education. The *Brown v. Board of Education* decision leveled the playing field. It also provided a legal basis for ending segregation in other public arenas.

Affirmative Action Programs and Their Foundations

In the mid-twentieth century, public universities started using programs known as "affirmative action" in their decisions about who should attend the university. The schools considered race and other parts of applicants' identities in their decisions about whether or not to admit each applicant. The programs had several purposes. Mostly they were a way to help minority applicants. In the United States, minorities have historically experienced discrimination, or different treatment, based on their identities. Affirmative action programs helped minorities gain access to better schools and work opportunities.

These programs have a long history in the United States. After the Civil War, the federal government created the Freedmen's Bureau. The bureau offered training and jobs to recently freed slaves. This was one of several programs that

President Lyndon Johnson shakes hands with Dr. Martin Luther King Jr. after signing the Civil Rights Act of 1964.

aimed to enforce the Fourteenth Amendment, passed in 1868. The amendment hoped to provide equal protection under the law for all American citizens, regardless of race. This meant that the states and the federal government could not treat minority citizens differently. The amendment also protected these people's right to due process. Due process is the right to receive the same legal treatment as every other American in the courts.

Unfortunately, some Supreme Court rulings in the late 1800s undermined the Fourteenth Amendment. In the *Civil Rights Cases* (1883), the Supreme Court ruled that the Civil Rights Act of 1875, which prohibited discrimination in public spaces, was unconstitutional. The court stated that the law allowed the government to be too involved in the ways in which states were able to treat their citizens. Similarly, the Supreme Court's ruling in cases like *Plessy v. Ferguson* (1896), which upheld the legality of segregated train cars, made way for legal segregation in the United States. These decisions were made around the same time that funding for programs like the Freedmen's Bureau was cut.

Public opinion started to change in the twentieth century. The federal government began to take an active role in undoing the damages of segregation. Chief Justice, or head judge of the United States Supreme Court, Earl Warren's 1954 decision in *Brown v. Board* made segregation of public schools unconstitutional. This was an important first step, but it took a national movement to make bigger changes.

The civil rights movement was led by figures like Dr. Martin Luther King Jr., Stokely Carmichael, Malcolm X, John Lewis, and Angela Davis. The movement led to the Civil Rights Act of 1964. This act promised protection of legal equality by the federal government. It also created the Equal Employment Opportunity Commission. This commission aimed at promoting and ensuring fair hiring and work treatment practices. The civil rights movement also led to the Voting Rights Act of 1965. This act protected political and voting rights for African Americans under national law. After the government was pushed to change by its people, it began to create institutions that protected all Americans from discrimination.

Affirmative action programs were developed throughout the 1960s and 1970s. In 1965, President Lyndon Johnson spoke on the subject of equal opportunities for African Americans. Johnson stated:

> Freedom is not enough. You do not wipe away the scars
> of centuries by saying: Now you are free to go where

you want, and do as you desire ... You do not take a
person who, for years, has been hobbled by chains
and liberate him, bring him up to the starting line of
a race and then say, "you are free to compete with all
the others," and still justly believe that you have been
completely fair. Thus it is not enough just to open the
gates of opportunity.

Johnson believed that ending segregation was not enough. He believed that opportunities needed to be created for minorities so that minorities could compete fairly. This speech reflected the growing desire for the government to ensure, by law, equal treatment for all citizens.

Affirmative action programs would begin to provide resources and protections that supported groups that had been victims of oppression. In 1965, Martin Luther King Jr. voiced his support for such programs. In an interview with journalist Alex Haley, King explained:

Few people reflect [on the fact] that for two centuries
the Negro was enslaved, and robbed of any wages—
potential accrued wealth which would have been the
legacy of his descendants. All of America's wealth
today could not adequately compensate its Negroes for
his centuries of exploitation and humiliation.

In other words, King believed that there was no amount of money in the world that could make up for the ways that slavery still affected African Americans. He believed that more needed to be done to help African Americans. The nation's leaders and activists agreed.

The University of California at Davis instituted an affirmative action program that would become the center of a national legal debate.

Regents of the University of California v. Bakke

In the 1970s, the School of Medicine at the University of California at Davis created a program it believed would give more opportunities to minorities. This program would also mean there would be more students from different backgrounds in the classrooms.

The system for choosing which students to admit to the university automatically rejected any student who applied who had a grade point average below 2.5 on a 4.0 scale. After that, there was a list of standards an admissions team used to evaluate the students. This list looked at students' interviews, grade point averages, scores on standardized tests, after-school activities, and letters from their teachers. The applicants were scored using these standards. After they were scored, the team either accepted or rejected the applicant.

Affirmative Action:
Regents of the University of California v. Bakke

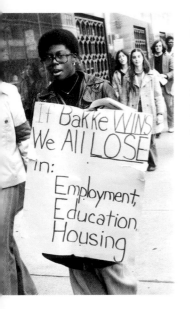

An affirmative action activist urges the courts not to side with Allan Bakke.

Students who said they belonged to a minority group or came from a place with limited opportunities did not have to meet the same standards. For instance, they did not need to have a 2.5 grade point average. Sixteen of the one hundred slots available at the school were set aside for these minority applicants. Sometimes these students were invited to attend the university using lower standards than other nonminority applicants.

In 1973 and 1974, a white applicant named Allan Bakke was denied admission to the University of California. Both times, minority applicants with lower overall scores received admission. Bakke felt like this was not fair and sued, or took legal action against, the university. He argued that the school had violated the Civil Rights Act of 1964 and the Fourteenth Amendment's equal protection clause. Both of these laws were created to keep minorities from being treated unfairly and discriminated against. Bakke claimed that the university was discriminating against him because he was white. He stated that he would probably have been admitted if he had been a person of color because his scores were higher than the minority applicants' scores. The University of California disagreed and defended its program. The program existed to provide opportunities for people who had been disadvantaged for centuries. The university also argued that there were many benefits to inviting minority applicants because of their diverse backgrounds.

The case sparked a national conversation about fairness, opportunity, and race that continues today. When the Supreme Court agreed to hear the case, it realized that it would make a decision that would establish the government's role in protecting minorities and equality. The case presented many complicated questions about the Constitution. The court's decision would offer complicated answers that would also create new questions.

Affirmative Action in America

Top universities started using affirmative action programs to make their student populations more diverse. The government made this possible. In 1961, President John F. Kennedy's Executive Order 10925 created the first official "affirmative action" program. The order required all government organizations to "take affirmative action to ensure that applicants are employed, and that employees are treated during employment, without regard to their race, creed, color, or national origin." For the first time, the government wanted to make sure that all individuals were treated fairly, regardless of their backgrounds. Public universities receive money from government organizations. This executive order meant that public universities could use affirmative action programs to invite more minorities to be a part of the university.

TWO

Challenging Affirmative Action in the Courts

Cases only reach the Supreme Court of the United States after a long process of review and appeals, or requests for a higher court to hear a case after a lower court makes a decision. If the case is an issue of federal law, or law related to the US government, then it goes before the federal court system. The federal court system includes district courts, the courts of appeals, and the Supreme Court. A district court or a court of appeals must hear the case before it is heard by the Supreme Court. A case only goes before the Supreme Court when the case deals with the way we understand the Constitution.

Cases that start in state courts must go through the state court system. In California, cases start in county superior courts. After the superior court, the case can be appealed to one of the state courts of appeals. If the plaintiff, the party bringing the legal challenge, or the defendant, the party defending the action or issue, is still not happy with the court's decision, then either party can appeal to the Supreme Court of California. In some cases, if one party is still not pleased, then the party can appeal to the US Supreme Court. The Supreme Court of the United States is made up of a

The Supreme Court of the United States hears issues of national legal importance in the courtroom pictured here.

chief justice and eight associate justices, or judges who are not the chief justice. All of the members of the Supreme Court are selected by the president. The US Senate has to approve the president's selections.

If the case is given a writ of certiorari, or an official declaration, then the Supreme Court will hear the case. *Regents of the University of California v. Bakke* went through the entire state system before being heard at the national level.

The History of Affirmative Action Lawsuits

Before Allan Bakke sued the University of California, the University of Washington's School of Law faced a similar legal battle. Marco DeFunis was a white male graduate of the University of Washington. He went on to apply to the university's law school. The law school's admissions team used three main standards to decide which applicants should be offered admission. The team scored the students on their academic achievements, their ability to be good classroom and community citizens, and their backgrounds. Students from certain racial backgrounds did not have to meet the same standards for academic success as nonminority students. DeFunis was rejected in 1971, even though he had scored higher than thirty-eight admitted minority applicants. He believed he had been unfairly denied acceptance, so he sued the school. In the Washington state courts, DeFunis argued that the special treatment given to minority applicants went against the Fourteenth Amendment's promise of equal protection.

The Washington Superior Court of King County agreed with DeFunis at first. He was admitted to the University of Washington's School of Law. The Washington Supreme Court reversed this decision. It believed that it was legal to deny some applicants like DeFunis to make room for less qualified students from different backgrounds. The court believed it was OK because the program encouraged integration, or the process of bringing groups previously segregated into shared spaces with shared resources. The decision set a precedent, or a legal standard based on previous cases, that schools could use these kinds of admissions programs if the programs were meant to promote school diversity. DeFunis was not pleased. He decided to appeal the decision to the US Supreme Court.

DeFunis was in his final year of law school when the case finally reached the US Supreme Court. The court listened to arguments from both sides. The justices decided that the legal question DeFunis raised was "moot," or unnecessary, in their per curiam, or collective, opinion. It did not matter how the court ruled because DeFunis was going to finish his degree at the University of Washington anyway. This response meant that the court did not decide whether or not affirmative action programs were legal. The justices left the door open to future challenges of affirmative action programs.

Several of the justices argued that the Supreme Court should have issued a more definitive ruling. They were correct.

The case of Allan Bakke (*center*) drew national media attention.

Bakke's Case and the Fourteenth Amendment

In 1962, Allan Bakke graduated from the University of Minnesota with a degree in mechanical engineering. He had a 3.51 out of 4.0 grade point average, was an honor student, and was a member of the US Navy's Reserve Officer Training Corps at the university. After earning his master's degree, he developed an interest in medicine. He decided to make a career switch. He applied to medical school at the University of California at Davis in 1972. He was rejected. After Bakke applied and was denied again in 1973, he began to consider legal action.

Bakke's lawyer, Reynold H. Colvin, filed a suit with the Yolo County California Superior Court in 1974. According to Colvin, the University of California had violated Bakke's Fourteenth Amendment right to equal protection. The equal protection clause states that "no state shall … deny to any person … the equal protection of the laws." In other words, the clause meant that all citizens should be treated the same under the law.

In 1954, the Supreme Court had determined in *Brown v. Board of Education of Topeka* that preventing African Americans from attending schools with whites was unconstitutional. In the ruling, Chief Justice Earl Warren wrote that education was "a right which must be made available to all on equal terms." Bakke argued that if unfairly treating minority students based on race was unconstitutional, then treating nonminority students differently based on race was also unconstitutional.

The University of California's admissions process went against Bakke's understanding of the equal protection clause. The school held 16 percent of the spots for minority students in the admissions process. The university reviewed applications of minority and nonminority students separately. The standards for admission for minority candidates were less selective. For example, a nonminority student would be automatically rejected if he or she had a grade point average lower than 2.5. There was no minimum grade point average requirement for minority students. Bakke and Colvin argued that the school was harder on Bakke because of his race. They argued that this was a violation of the clause.

The President and Congress Weigh In on Affirmative Action

A t the time that Bakke's case was making its way to the Supreme Court, the Democratic majority in Congress and President Jimmy Carter, also a Democrat, both strongly encouraged affirmative action programs. Both branches of government agreed that these programs did not violate the equal protection clause of the Fourteenth Amendment. President Carter stated that he had "been strongly committed to a policy of affirmative action." He believed that "through such programs ... we can expect to remove the effects of discrimination and ensure equal opportunities for all Americans." The Carter administration submitted an amicus curiae brief to the Supreme Court about the *Bakke* case. The brief argued that the affirmative action program was constitutional. The attorney general, or the chief lawyer of the United States, Griffin Bell, worked with the solicitor general, or the lawyer responsible for arguing cases before the United States Supreme Court, Wade H. McCree, to write the document.

In the county court, Judge F. Leslie Manker decided that the university's program was a violation of the Fourteenth Amendment in 1974. He argued that "the use of this program did substantially reduce [the] plaintiff's chances of successful admission ... No race or ethnic group should ever be granted privileges or immunities not given to every other race." However, Manker did not force the school to admit Bakke. He simply made the school reconsider Bakke's application without considering his race. He also later demanded that the university never use race as a factor in the application process. The Regents, or governing board members, of the University of California were not pleased with this decision. The university decided to appeal the case to the Supreme Court of California.

The state's highest court heard arguments in the case in 1976. Nine separate organizations filed amicus curiae

The Earl Warren Building houses the Supreme Court of California.

Bakke's case sparked national protests about affirmative action programs.

briefs, or opinions on the case written by groups interested in influencing the justices' decisions. The Supreme Court of California agreed with the lower court's ruling after hearing arguments and deliberating for six months. The court ruled 6–1 that the university's program went against the equal protection clause. The court agreed that the affirmative action program was unconstitutional. It also ruled that the university had to accept Bakke unless it could prove that Bakke was unacceptable for admission when his race was not considered. The university decided to appeal the ruling to the Supreme Court of the United States. Justice William Rehnquist of the US Supreme Court stopped Bakke's admission to the University of California so that the court could review the case. Two short years after the Supreme Court justices avoided a decision in Marco DeFunis's case, they prepared to look again at affirmative action.

THREE

The Supreme Court and *Regents of the University of California v. Bakke*

The Supreme Court gathered on October 12, 1977, to hear oral arguments for *Regents of the University of California v. Bakke.* In general, the Supreme Court only agrees to hear cases that raise significant constitutional questions. In other words, the court asks if a case requires a new interpretation of the US Constitution. In *Bakke,* there were two key questions to answer about the Constitution. Was the University of California violating Allan Bakke's right, under the Fourteenth Amendment, to "equal protection"? Additionally, was the University of California violating his protections against discrimination outlined in the Civil Rights Act of 1964 by denying him admission because of his race?

The Laws in Question

The Fourteenth Amendment to the Constitution and the Civil Rights Act of 1964 were the two laws in question. In 1868, the Fourteenth Amendment was added to the Constitution to answer important questions about American society after the end of slavery. It explained how former

President Jimmy Carter supported affirmative action programs.

slaves should be treated under the law. The first section states that all people born in the United States should be considered citizens. This section also ensures that the states cannot violate any citizen's rights protected under the Bill of Rights, federal law, or state law without due process, or a fair trial. Finally, the states must apply the laws equally without advantaging or disadvantaging one group of citizens over another. This final part of the Fourteenth Amendment is known as the equal protection clause. Bakke felt this right had been violated by the university.

The second piece of law in question was the Civil Rights Act of 1964. The specific part in question was Title VI:

> No person in the United States shall, on the ground of race, color, or national origin, be excluded from participation in, be denied the benefits of, or be subjected to discrimination under any program or activity receiving Federal financial assistance.

Bakke and Colvin argued that the university's program went against Title VI. The University of California is a public university. Public universities receive government funding. Colvin believed Bakke had specifically been excluded from the university because of his race, which meant Title VI of the Civil Rights Act had been violated.

Is Discrimination Ever Legal?

Discrimination is illegal under these laws in question and other federal laws. The government does, however, discriminate, or judge, in some instances. In *Bakke*, the University of California argued that discrimination was allowed because the university was trying to create a student body with people from different backgrounds. The university was also trying to make up for injustices against African Americans. The courts at all levels agreed that some discrimination takes place when a college decides which students to admit.

A public institution must prove that there is a rational basis for the discrimination if it wants to treat people differently. The "rational basis test" means that there has to be a "legitimate state interest." In other words, there must be a logical connection between what the goals are and how the goals are to be achieved. In college admissions, there must be a rational connection between what the university's goals are and how it goes about achieving them. For instance, state universities can easily prove the need to discriminate based on academic standards. One of the institution's goals is to have a strong academic profile. It then makes sense for a school to reject someone with lower test scores. This person with low scores may have a negative effect on the school's academic profile.

The law requires something different when considering racial discrimination. The law requires this type of discrimination to pass the "strict scrutiny test." This means an institution can only discriminate if it proves that the discrimination serves a "compelling governmental interest"— in other words, a really important goal. Additionally, the institution must demonstrate that its particular policy is carefully defined and is the best way to achieve that goal. In the *Bakke* case, the school needed to prove that discriminating against white students was the best way of achieving its goal of diversity.

The Plaintiff, Its Lawyers, and Their Arguments

The University of California at Davis served as the plaintiff when the case went before the Supreme Court. The plaintiff is the party or group in a lawsuit that is challenging the court's decision or the law in place. Allan Bakke was the plaintiff when the case was before the California state courts.

Affirmative Action:
Regents of the University of California v. Bakke

The university was the plaintiff before the United States Supreme Court because the school was trying to prove that the California courts made a mistake when they decided that Bakke was a victim of discrimination. This meant that Bakke was now the defendant. The university hired Archibald Cox, a former solicitor general, as its lawyer. Cox was helped by the current solicitor general, Wade H. McCree.

Cox's argument focused on the legal issues. He rarely mentioned Bakke by name. Cox emphasized the university's freedom to select which students it accepted. He argued that the affirmative action process was necessary in order to invite students from different backgrounds to the university. He also argued that the program was necessary to correct for past harms done to minorities. In order to pass the strict scrutiny test, he needed to argue that these were necessary goals. Cox also stated that there was "no racially blind method of selection which will enroll today more than a trickle of minority students in the nation's colleges and professions." In other words, these programs were necessary because there would be no other way to give these minorities fair access to education and work opportunities.

Justice Lewis F. Powell Jr. responded by asking Cox about the admissions quota, or a set number, for minority students. Powell noted that the University of California set aside sixteen spots for minority students. The justice also noted that Bakke could not be considered for those spots because he was white. He asked Cox if that was discrimination against nonminority students. Cox responded by stating that the Constitution did not ban this kind of discrimination. Cox argued that "the Fourteenth Amendment does not outlaw race-conscious programs … aimed at offsetting the consequences of our long, tragic history of discrimination." In other words, the program was legal if it helped students who came from populations that had been discriminated against in the past. Cox stated that that was the original intention of the Fourteenth Amendment.

Wade McCree was the second African American US solicitor general.

Associate counsel Wade McCree argued further for the university. McCree argued that the Constitution itself contained racially discriminatory principles. The three-fifths clause allowed slave states in the 1800s to count slaves in the state's population for representation purposes. In the clause, each slave was considered "three fifths of all other persons" in the population count. This clause did not require the states to treat the slaves as citizens. This meant that the state did

The 1978 Supreme Court justices: (*clockwise from top left*) Rehnquist, Blackmun, Powell, Stevens, Marshall, Stewart, Burger, Brennan, White

not have to give slaves constitutional rights. McCree argued that this was an example of discrimination. Similarly, the fugitive slave clause required the return of runaway slaves. Elsewhere, the Constitution also required that the slave trade continue for twenty years after the document's ratification, or official signing. Again, McCree argued that this clause was discriminatory. McCree argued that affirmative action programs were made to assist "persons who were held back"

Archibald Cox: A Legal Legend

The University of California hired one of the nation's most famous attorneys: Archibald Cox. Cox had served as an assistant to Solicitor General Charles Fahy. After, President Harry Truman appointed Cox to head the Wage Stabilization Board. He soon quit this job to return to teaching at Harvard University. Cox advised Senator John F. Kennedy while in Massachusetts. After Kennedy was elected president, Cox served on his presidential advisory team. Eventually, Kennedy appointed Cox solicitor general. In this position, he worked with Attorney General Robert Kennedy to write and enforce civil rights laws like the Voting Rights Act of 1965. In 1973, Cox became special prosecutor for the Watergate investigation. The investigation explored whether or not President Richard Nixon illegally spied on his political opponents. Cox asked the Supreme Court to force Nixon to turn over White House tape recordings. Nixon had Cox fired. Later, Nixon was forced to release the tapes. He eventually stepped down from the presidency.

As an experienced attorney, Cox used his knowledge of the government and civil rights to argue for the University of California's affirmative action program.

by clauses like these. If the programs were made to do that, then they must be legal under the Fourteenth Amendment and the Civil Rights Act of 1964.

McCree and Cox both asked one fundamental question. If both laws existed to help give fair chances to all people, then how could a program that does that be banned by the same laws?

Chief Justice Burger asked the attorneys if there was any evidence that the school had excluded or discriminated against anyone on the basis of race. Both lawyers responded that there was not any. At its core, the program existed to help people of minority backgrounds. It did not exclude people who were not minorities.

The Defendant, His Lawyer, and His Argument

Bakke's lawyer addressed the justices after McCree and Cox finished their arguments. Reynold H. Colvin was far less experienced than the other lawyers. He used most of his time to discuss the case's background information. Colvin finally argued that Bakke was the victim of an illegal quota when the justices asked him to focus on the constitutional question. He argued that a system that set aside slots for minority students excluded anyone who was not a minority. He argued that that sort of system went against both Title VI and the equal protection clause. Colvin stated that Bakke was being treated unfairly because he was white. Justice Potter Stewart asked Colvin if anyone had the "right to be admitted" to a school. Colvin responded that Bakke did not have a right to be admitted. He instead argued that Bakke had a right not to be discriminated against while applying.

Warren E. Burger was the chief justice of the US Supreme Court from 1969 to 1986.

Allan Bakke believed the University of California denied him admission because of his race.

Colvin's insistence that a race-based quota was unfair to nonminority students led to a testy conversation with Justice Thurgood Marshall, the first African American to serve on the Supreme Court:

The Supreme Court and *Regents of the University of California v. Bakke*

Marshall: Your client did compete for the eighty-four seats [not reserved for minorities], didn't he?

Colvin: Yes, he did.

Marshall: And he lost ... Now would your argument be the same if one instead of sixteen seats were left open [to minorities]? ...

Colvin: Yes ... whether it is one, one hundred, two ... The numbers are not important. It is the principle of keeping a man out because of his race that is important ...

Marshall: You are talking about your client's rights. Don't these underprivileged people have some rights?

Colvin: They certainly have the right to compete—

Marshall: To eat cake.

Colvin: They have the right to compete. They have the right to equal competition.

Colvin argued that any use of race in the admissions process was discrimination. He did not believe these programs trying to help minorities were legal under Title VI.

The justices gathered to consider the details of the case after the lawyers gave their arguments. The court's justices went over the wording of each law. They studied the details of the University of California's affirmative action program. The justices also read about previous Supreme Court decisions on similar cases. In the end, they had to decide whether or not affirmative action programs were constitutional.

FOUR

The Court Debates and Issues a Ruling

The Supreme Court justices enter a conference session after hearing oral arguments. Here, the justices debate the merits of each argument. They decide which views are in the majority. Then, the chief justice assigns opinion-writing tasks to the various justices. These opinions express the different views of different justices. The conference session following the oral arguments in the *Bakke* case was long and deliberative.

Each justice had a different perspective on the issues of the case. Each justice also had different reasons for his position. Justice William Brennan argued that the use of race in this context was in line with the original purpose of the equal protection clause. Justice Byron White argued that Title VI did not apply here because the law was meant to help minorities. He believed the university's admission program aimed to do that. Justice Marshall argued that the university's quota system was not meant to exclude people. He believed it was created to forcibly include people. Chief Justice Burger believed that diversity could be achieved through other, better means. He did not believe that medical schools like the University of California at Davis should be responsible

Conference sessions happen in rooms like the East Conference Room in the Supreme Court Building.

for this task. Justice Stewart and Justice Rehnquist took this a step further. They argued that "no state agency can take race into account" because the equal protection clause banned any sort of negative treatment on the basis of race. Justice John Paul Stevens agreed but argued that affirmative action should, in theory, be a temporary program. He hoped for a day when these programs would no longer be necessary. Justice Powell added that the university had made a mistake in setting a quota. He believed diversity was an important task for the school, but setting a minimum number of admitted minority students was wrong.

Justice Lewis F. Powell wrote the majority opinion, which made racial quotas illegal.

On June 28, 1978, the Supreme Court of the United States gave its ruling in *Regents of the University of California v. Bakke*. The ruling was complex and made up of many parts. It did not put the issue of affirmative

33

action to bed. It actually set a legal basis for future disputes over the issue.

The Questions at Hand

The decision looked to answer four key legal questions. First, did Allan Bakke have grounds to sue in the first place? The Supreme Court needed to decide if there had been a violation of his rights guaranteed by Title VI of the Civil Rights Act of 1964. Second, did the same act make the University of California's affirmative action policy illegal? The justices examined whether or not Title VI meant that any discrimination on the basis of race was illegal. Third, was Bakke's rejection a violation of his rights under the equal protection clause? Finally, were any race-based affirmative action programs legal? Ultimately, the court needed to consider if the language of the Civil Rights Act and the Fourteenth Amendment were meant to protect all individuals or just minorities.

Although the justices had very different interpretations, a majority agreed on the answers to the four questions outlined above. First, Bakke did have grounds to sue under the Civil Rights Act. He was arguing that his civil rights had been violated based on his race. Second, the same law did not permit admissions programs to use race as the only determining factor for admission. The court determined this using the strict scrutiny test. The court did rule, however, that the equal protection clause allowed universities to consider race as one of several factors for admission. Finally, this interpretation meant that while some affirmative action programs were constitutional, others were not. The affirmative action program created by the University of California was

Justices and Their Votes

Question 1: Did the Civil Rights Act provide Bakke a cause of action to sue?
Yes: Burger, Brennan, Stewart, Marshall, Blackmun, Powell, Rehnquist, Stevens
No: White

Question 2: Did the Civil Rights Act prohibit the university's race-based admissions program?
Yes: Burger, Stewart, Rehnquist, Stevens
No: Brennan, White, Marshall, Blackmun, Powell

Question 3: Does the equal protection clause permit race to be one factor, among many, in an admissions program?
Yes: Brennan, White, Marshall, Blackmun, Powell
No: Burger, Stewart, Rehnquist, Stevens

Question 4: Does the equal protection clause prohibit the university's specific race-based admissions program, and should Bakke be admitted?
Yes: Burger, Stewart, Powell, Rehnquist, Stevens
No: Brennan, White, Marshall, Blackmun

Since the justices were so divided on affirmative action, they decided to publish six different opinions.

not constitutional because of its use of racial quotas. Racial quotas meant that race was the primary determining factor.

The Majority Opinion

The majority opinion, or the written explanation of a court's ruling in a case, was complicated and controversial. Justice Powell wrote this opinion with Chief Justice Burger and Associate Justices Stewart, Rehnquist, and Stevens. Stevens also wrote a separate opinion to explain why he sided with the majority on most of its ruling. Justices Brennan, White, Marshall, and Harry Blackmun all filed separate opinions that mostly disagreed with the majority.

Powell's majority opinion concluded that Bakke had suffered from discrimination at the hands of the University of California. He argued that the strict scrutiny test applied in this case. This meant that the university first needed to prove that it had a convincing reason for affirmative action programs. The university then needed to prove that affirmative action programs were the best way of achieving that goal. Powell stated that "the court agreed that the goals of integrating the medical profession and increasing the number of physicians willing to serve members of minority groups were compelling state interests." In other words, the majority of the justices agreed that it was important to have people of different background at the medical school. These people from different backgrounds could serve patients of different backgrounds. The problem was that the court did not agree that affirmative action programs were the best way of achieving diversity. The majority of the justices thought there were better ways to integrate the medical school that did not go against the equal protection clause. Powell wrote

Protesters wanted the precedent established in *Bakke* to be expanded.

that the language of the Fourteenth Amendment meant that "no applicant may be rejected because of his race."

Specifically, the court ruled that the university's quota system was the problem. Powell argued that "whether this limitation is described as a quota or a goal, it is a line drawn on the basis of race and ethnic status." This line was a violation of the Fourteenth Amendment. Powell went on to say that the "guarantee of equal protection cannot mean

Protesters rallied against the US Supreme Court's decision.

one thing when applied to one individual and something else when applied to a person of another color." The majority ruled that the University of California at Davis had used a program that violated the equal protection clause. The program also went against Title VI of the Civil Rights Act. The majority ruled that Bakke should be admitted.

The court did not rule against all affirmative action programs. Powell argued that "ethnic diversity … is only one element in a range of factors a university properly may consider in attaining the goal of a heterogeneous student body." In other words, affirmative action programs that were

38

not based on quotas were constitutional. The justices agreed that schools can consider race as one of many other factors when determining who to invite into the university. Race just cannot be the only factor that the school considers.

Powell's opinion was a middle ground between the two opposing groups. Justices Stevens, Stewart, Rehnquist, and Burger only somewhat agreed with Powell's opinion. Together they wrote a separate, more specific one. These four justices argued there was no need for a review of the equal protection clause. The clause didn't need to be reviewed because the affirmative action program went against Title VI. The university broke the law when it rejected Bakke because of his race. These justices argued that the university went against the Civil Rights Act of 1964. This violation meant that the court did not also need to consider the equal protection clause because the law was already broken. The justices argued that "nothing in the legislative history justifies" the protection of only minorities under the Civil Rights Act. Stevens argued that the law existed to prevent any form of discrimination.

Dissenting Opinions

Justices Brennan, White, Marshall, and Blackmun cowrote an opinion that agreed with Powell's argument that race could be used in admissions processes. Their dissenting opinion, or written explanation that did not side with the majority, disagreed with almost everything else the majority argued. These justices argued that the affirmative action program at Davis Medical School was constitutional. The justices based this opinion on the history of the Fourteenth Amendment and the Civil Rights Act. They stated that it was OK for the school to treat applicants of different races separately. They said this treatment was acceptable because it was meant to help disadvantaged populations. The justices argued that Title VI was meant to protect minorities. Title VI was also meant to help people recover from past inequalities. The law was "not to demean or insult any racial group, but to remedy disadvantages cast on minorities by past racial prejudice." In other words, the law only meant to uplift those who were previously treated unfairly.

All of these justices also wrote their own separate opinions. Justice Blackmun argued that universities already gave exceptions to all sorts of groups. He said that athletes, children of alums, and the rich and famous get special treatment. If it was legal to give these groups special treatment, then why was it illegal to give minorities special

Justice Thurgood Marshall wrote a moving opinion on the need for race-conscious admissions policies.

treatment? Justice Blackmun also argued that it was OK for universities to use quotas if all applicants were being reviewed by similar standards. Similarly, Justice White argued that the Civil Rights Act was meant to help minorities. White believed the law had not been created to protect someone like Bakke.

In the most passionate opinion, Justice Thurgood Marshall wrote on the history of race in the United States. Marshall was the first African American to hold the position of solicitor general. He was also the first African

American Supreme Court justice. Marshall explained that the government needed to support programs like the University of California's.

Marshall pointed out that Congress, past presidents, and the Supreme Court had passed laws and government policies that discriminated against and disadvantaged African Americans. He pointed out the racial discrimination present

Chief Justice Warren E. Burger

President Richard Nixon appointed Chief Justice Warren E. Burger in 1969. Burger was a conservative, but he oversaw significant liberal-leaning decisions by the court. He began his political career working for the Republican Party in Minnesota. In 1953, President Dwight Eisenhower selected him for a position in the Justice Department. Burger was then selected to join the District of Columbia Federal Circuit Court of Appeals in 1956. He served as chief justice of the Supreme Court for seventeen years. During this time, he was "cautiously conservative." This meant that he was more interested in following the letter of the law than his political leanings. For instance, the court often supported increased civil liberties and rights. Burger had not supported these policies before becoming chief justice. Rulings like this showed how Burger's understanding of the Constitution often reflected the same middle-ground position he took in the *Bakke* case.

in the Declaration of Independence. The document stating that "all men are created equal" had been written by Thomas Jefferson. Jefferson owned slaves, so he did not believe all men of all races were created equal. Marshall also pointed out how the three-fifths clause in the Constitution protected slavery. In other words, the country's past laws created the issues that minorities were facing.

Marshall stated that it was "more than a little ironic that, after several hundred years of class-based discrimination against Negroes, the Court is unwilling to hold that a class-based remedy for that discrimination is permissible." In other words, he found it odd that institutions responsible for the oppression were now refusing to support a program that aimed to fix the problems they had created. Programs like the University of California's admissions program created chances for people who previously did not have them. Marshall warned that ending these programs would reduce equal opportunities for many African Americans.

Some Answers and More Questions

The court had ruled, but not with a single voice. The decision meant that people could continue to question specific affirmative action programs at specific universities. If Davis's program was unconstitutional and others were not, it would take additional rulings to decide whether or not each program was constitutional. Although *Bakke* was a landmark case for the Supreme Court, it did not end the debate over affirmative action. The conversation was just beginning.

FIVE

The Impact of the *Bakke* Ruling

Affirmative action programs have a long history in the United States. They date as far back as the post–Civil War Reconstruction Era. In Justice Marshall's dissenting opinion in the *Bakke* case, he argued that the government had allowed these types of programs before. Marshall stated that "Congress responded to legal disabilities being imposed [on African Americans] … by establishing … the Freedmen's Bureau, to supply food, hospitals, land, and education to the newly freed slaves." Marshall argued that the government had created a precedent for programs like affirmative action. The Civil Rights Act of 1964 and the Voting Rights Act of 1965 created legal barriers to discrimination.

Presidential Stances on Affirmative Action

The implementation of those barriers became the responsibility of the executive branch. The executive branch is made up of the president, vice president, the cabinet, and several other departments. Each president and executive branch have dealt with affirmative action differently. The first significant affirmative action program came under

President Richard Nixon. He built on President Lyndon
B. Johnson's Executive Order 11246, which required
government contractors to "take affirmative action" and
aimed at establishing a system of nondiscriminatory hiring
practices for them. Johnson's order, however, lacked specific
regulations. Nixon developed them. In 1969, Nixon issued
the "Philadelphia Order," which imposed specific goals
and deadlines on federal contractors for hiring minority
employees. Although the "Philadelphia Order" was initially
challenged, the courts upheld that it was constitutional.

President Jimmy Carter also supported affirmative action
programs. As president during the *Bakke* case, Carter allowed
the Department of Justice to help the University of California
make its case. He selected Solicitor General Wade McCree
to be a lawyer for the university. He also publicly stated, after
the court's ruling, that he was "strongly committed to a policy
of affirmative action."

In 1980, Ronald Reagan defeated Jimmy Carter's
presidential reelection attempt. After that, the tides
shifted. In 1981, the *New York Times* reported that the
Reagan White House was opposed "to affirmative action
hiring programs." Reagan disliked quota systems like
the University of California's. In a 1985 address, Reagan
stated that "quotas deny jobs to many who would have
gotten them otherwise." He even warned that quotas "cast
a shadow on the real achievements of minorities, which
makes quotas a double tragedy." In his administration,
Reagan removed federal protections for programs that
had quota systems. His reasoning was that these programs
discriminated against nonminorities and stole the spotlight
from high-achieving minorities.

Jennifer Gratz (*right*) and Barbara Grutter (*left*) both sued the University of Michigan.

George H. W. Bush, Reagan's vice president and then presidential successor, also opposed many affirmative action programs. In the second year of his term as president, Bush did not support the Civil Rights Act of 1990. This act made sure that employers could not discriminate against minorities. Bush defended his position. He said that the law had a quota system. He believed this system did more harm than good. The law's defenders felt similarly to the lawyers representing the University of California. Senator Edward Kennedy called Bush's lack of support "tragic and disgraceful." Bush responded by stating that his administration was "committed to action that is truly affirmative, positive action in every sense, to strike down all barriers to advancement of every kind for all people." By this, Bush meant he only supported affirmative action programs that did not just support minorities. Bush eventually signed a different version of the Civil Rights Act into law after facing pressure from Congress in 1991.

President Bill Clinton, Bush's successor, again felt differently. He declared that affirmative action programs were "good for America." Clinton committed the government to supporting these policies. In a 1995 speech, Clinton stated that "in the fight for the future, we need all hands on deck.

And some of those hands still need a helping hand." In other words, in order for everyone to move forward, there must be a level playing field for all citizens. Clinton's successor, President George W. Bush, saw things differently. He argued that some methods of affirmative action were "fundamentally flawed." In 2003, Bush stated that "a quota system … unfairly rewards or penalizes prospective students, based solely on their race." This meant that he saw these systems as discriminatory.

President Barack Obama disagreed with his predecessor. In 2014, he declaring that affirmative action programs using quotas were acceptable. He argued that schools should be allowed to consider race if the interest is compelling enough. Obama stated that these programs were legal "if [a school] decides that there is a value in making sure that folks with different experiences in a classroom will enhance the educational experience of the students, and they do it in a careful way."

President Donald Trump also disagrees with his predecessor. Trump has asked the Justice Department to investigate "intentional race-based discrimination in college and university admissions." In this instance, the president wants to explore if affirmative action programs discriminate against nonminorities.

Although most presidents have had different feelings about affirmative action, the Supreme Court has worked to develop an understanding over time.

The Supreme Court's Rulings on Affirmative Action Before and After *Bakke*

Before Allan Bakke's case, the Supreme Court had not made a decision on any other affirmative action cases. There was no

precedent because the court had not
made a decision in Marco DeFunis's
case. Luckily, the Supreme Court
had ruled on other cases that would
help it make its decision. It declared
segregation unconstitutional in *Brown
v. Board of Education of Topeka* (1954).
The court had also handled other
cases dealing with discrimination in
selection processes. For instance, the
court ruled that companies could not
discriminate against black employees
in hiring processes in *Griggs v. Duke
Power Company* (1971).

Jack Greenberg argued for
black employees in *Griggs
v. Duke Power Company.*

After *Regents of the University
of California v. Bakke*, the federal
courts had a precedent for future
rulings. In the 1996 case *Hopwood
v. University of Texas Law School*, the United States Court
of Appeals for the Fifth Circuit ruled that considering
race in admissions procedures was unconstitutional. This
decision was overturned, or reversed, by the Supreme Court
in 2003. In 2003, the court heard two cases that challenged
the University of Michigan's undergraduate and law school
admissions policies. The court ruled in *Gratz v. Bollinger*
that the school had violated the equal protection clause. The
school had admitted almost every minority undergraduate
applicant. The court decided that the university was not
considering each applicant individually. The precedent set in
Bakke meant this policy was illegal. The court ruled in *Grutter
v. Bollinger* that the law school's affirmative action program

was constitutional. This program looked at race as one of many elements of an applicant's qualifications. Again, this was a precedent set by the *Bakke* case.

Years after her case, Gratz continued to speak against affirmative action programs.

In 2013, the Supreme Court ruled in *Fisher v. University of Texas*. The decision meant that courts must use the strict scrutiny test when evaluating an affirmative action program. They must also use the strict scrutiny test when ruling on the program's constitutionality. The case was sent back to a lower court to be reargued with the strict scrutiny test in mind. Next, it was once again appealed to the Supreme Court as *Fisher v. University of Texas II*. In 2016, the Supreme Court ruled in favor of the University of Texas's admissions policy. The university had offered automatic acceptance to the top 10 percent of each Texas high school's graduating class. These acceptances did not consider race. The university then reserved spots for other highly qualified candidates. One of the factors admissions teams would consider for these other slots was race. Race was not the only factor they would consider. This policy did not violate the equal protection clause. It also did not violate the *Regents of the University of California v. Bakke* precedent. The Supreme Court ruled in favor of the university and upheld the lower court's ruling.

The *Regents of the University of California v. Bakke* decision created a precedent for affirmative action programs in

Abigail Noel Fisher (*right*) argued that the University of Texas's affirmative action policy violated her Fourteenth Amendment rights.

America. Even still, the debate over these programs continues. Many critics of the programs point to a phenomenon known as "mismatch," where students admitted to competitive universities through affirmative action programs do not succeed. The students are underqualified, underprepared, and underperforming. For that reason, critics of affirmative action do not believe students are benefiting from these programs. Justices Antonin Scalia and Clarence Thomas mentioned this phenomenon in the *Fisher* case. Supporters of this position do not suggest that minorities should not be admitted to top academic institutions. They just wonder if these programs are helping or hurting minority students.

Critics of the "mismatch" phenomenon say that there is no reason to believe that affirmative action is the cause of underperformance. A study done by researchers at the University of California, Davis, and the University of Wisconsin–Madison looked at grade point averages, credits, and dropout rates of accepted students from both the high and low ends of the applicant pool. At the end of these students' college careers, researchers concluded that students admitted from the lower end of the applicant pool to the more selective University of California schools only "were at a slight disadvantage relative to their better prepared peers." In other words, the students who had lower test scores in high school performed only at a slightly lower level than those with higher test scores. Despite the slight disadvantage, researcher Michal Kurlaender believes this data weakens the arguments against affirmative action programs that use the "mismatch" phenomenon as evidence. She argues that the study helps to demonstrate how "mismatched students are more likely to persist in college ... and do not pay a penalty in terms of grades for doing so." Ultimately, the verdict is still out about the effects of affirmative action programs.

Justice O'Connor (*right*), the first female Supreme Court justice, was sworn in by Chief Justice Burger (*left*) in 1981.

In 2003, Justice Sandra Day O'Connor wrote in the court's *Grutter v. Bollinger* opinion: "We expect that 25 years from now, the use of racial preferences will no longer be necessary to further the interest approved today." O'Connor supported the affirmative action program used by the University of Michigan. She also looked forward to a day when discrimination would no longer keep people from being treated fairly. O'Connor's vision has yet to be realized.

The United States has employed programs and resources to help correct inequality. Affirmative action programs strive to provide opportunities for Americans who are victims of those inequalities. The programs remain imperfect and controversial.

Debating *Bakke* and Affirmative Action Today

The *Regents of the University of California v. Bakke* case started a long-lasting debate about affirmative action programs. In 2014, an advocacy group, Students for Fair Admissions, representing Asian American applicants filed a lawsuit against Harvard University. In an article for the *New Yorker*, Harvard Law School Professor Jeannie Suk Gersen stated that "the lawsuit alleges that Harvard effectively employs quotas on the number of Asians admitted and holds them to a higher standard than whites." She goes on to write that "at selective colleges, Asians are demographically overrepresented minorities, but they are underrepresented relative to the applicant pool." In other words, the advocacy group is challenging the limited number of spots it believes that Harvard reserves for Asian American applicants. This quota means that many qualified Asian American applicants are not offered admission. Since Harvard University receives federal funding under Title VI of the Civil Rights Act of 1964 in order to promote diversity, the Justice Department is involved in the case. This investigation started around the same time that Attorney General Jeff Sessions announced that the Justice Department would investigate affirmative action programs, as he finds them "very troubling." The debate, it seems, will continue.

Chronology

- **1857** The Supreme Court rules all descendants of African slaves are not citizens, regardless of whether or not they are enslaved or free (*Dred Scott v. Sandford*).

- **1896** The Supreme Court rules that segregation of public entities is constitutional, establishing the "separate but equal" precedent (*Plessy v. Ferguson*).

- **1938** The Supreme Court rules states must provide educational opportunities for black and white students, even if schools remain segregated (*Missouri ex rel. Gaines v. Canada*).

- **1954** The Supreme Court rules that separate educational institutions are unconstitutional, ending segregation (*Brown v. Board of Education of Topeka*).

- **1961** President John F. Kennedy's issues Executive Order 10925, calling on government contractors to "take affirmative action to ensure that applicants are employed and ... treated ... without regard to their race, creed, color, or national origin."

1978 The Supreme Court rules race can be among several factors colleges consider when deciding which students they should admit (*Regents of the University of California v. Bakke*).

1996 The Court of Appeals for the Fifth Circuit bans racial considerations for admission; this is later qualified by the Supreme Court (*Hopwood v. University of Texas Law School*).

2003 The Supreme Court rules that the University of Michigan's undergraduate affirmative action program, which admitted nearly every minority applicant, violates the equal protection clause (*Gratz v. Bollinger*). The Supreme Court also decides that the University of Michigan's School of Law proved a substantial, compelling interest in promoting diversity, rendering its own, more limited affirmative action program constitutional (*Grutter v. Bollinger*).

2007 The Supreme Court rules that previous rulings on affirmative action do not apply to public high schools (*Parents v. Seattle*).

2016 The Supreme Court rules that the University of Texas's program, which offers automatic admission to the top 10 percent of each graduating class and considers race as a factor for other applicants, is constitutional (*Fisher v. University of Texas II*).

Glossary

amicus curiae brief A "friend of the court" brief, or a documentation submitted by interested parties to help influence justices and attorneys in a case.

appeal A request for a higher court to hear a case after the initial court makes its ruling.

associate justice of the Supreme Court A justice who serves on the court after being appointed by the president and confirmed by the Senate.

attorney general The head of the United States Department of Justice, who is the head lawyer of the United States and its government.

chief justice of the Supreme Court The justice who presides over the other justices and provides leadership in crafting opinions and rulings.

civil rights Rights and liberties protected for all groups under the law.

dissenting opinion The written explanation of a justice's decision to not side with the majority.

equal protection clause The part of the Fourteenth Amendment to the Constitution that demands all citizens be treated equally under the law.

executive order A presidential action, order, or initiative.

integration The process of bringing groups previously segregated into collective spaces with shared resources.

majority opinion The written explanation of the court's ruling in a case.

per curiam opinion A collective opinion issued by the court that is a general statement of law, rather than an individually composed legal opinion.

precedent The established norms and ideas from previous court cases that are used to inform current cases.

quota A set number of something, such as the University of California setting a minimum number of minority acceptances.

rational basis test The concept that the government must prove that it has a "legitimate government interest" in discriminating against one group or another. Generally, this standard is easier to prove than that of strict scrutiny.

segregation The legal and social separation of groups based on race.

solicitor general The lawyer who represents the federal government of the United States to the Supreme Court.

strict scrutiny test The concept that the government must prove that it has a "compelling interest" in order to discriminate against a group, such as a racial, religious, political, or national minority.

Title VI A section of the Civil Rights Act of 1964 that forbids discrimination by federally funded institutions on the basis of race, color, or national origin.

writ of certiorari The official, documented order that a case will be heard by the Supreme Court.

Further Information

Books

Anderson, Jerry H. *The Pursuit of Fairness: A History of Affirmative Action*. Oxford, UK: Oxford University Press, 2005.

Ball, Howard. *The Bakke Case: Race, Education, and Affirmative Action*. Lawrence: University of Kansas Press, 2000.

Fayer, Steve, and Henry Hampton. *Voices of Freedom: An Oral History of the Civil Rights Movement from the 1950s Through the 1980s*. London, UK: Bantam, 1991.

Guinier, Lani. *The Tyranny of the Meritocracy. Democratizing Higher Education in America*. Boston: Beacon Press, 2016.

Sowell, Thomas. *Affirmative Action Around the World*. New Haven, CT: Yale University Press, 2004.

Websites

The Legal Information Institute
https://www.law.cornell.edu

The institute's website provides access to legal collections.

Oyez

https://www.oyez.org

Oyez is a free multimedia collection that provides information about the Supreme Court.

Street Law

http://streetlaw.org/en

Street Law provides educational programs about the law and human rights.

Videos

Affirmative Action on Campus Does More Harm than Good

https://www.intelligencesquaredus.org/debates/affirmative-action-campus-does-more-harm-good

This debate focuses on whether or not affirmative action programs help or hurt students.

Debating Affirmative Action

https://constitutioncenter.org/blog/live-video-645-p-m-debating-affirmative-action

This debate discusses whether or not the equal protection clause prohibits admissions committees from considering race.

Eyes on the Prize: Episode 13: The Keys to the Kingdom (1974–1980)

https://www.youtube.com/watch?v=zn2-TT_Bk1M

This episode of the fourteen-part documentary series *Eyes on the Prize* looks at the *Bakke* case.

Selected Bibliography

Bodenhamer, David J. *Our Rights*. New York: Oxford University Press, 2007.

Bush, George W. "Bush's Statement on Affirmative Action." *New York Times*, January 15, 2003. http://www.nytimes.com/2003/01/15/politics/bushs-statement-on-affirmative-action.html.

Carter, James. "Affirmative Action Programs Memorandum from the President." The American Presidency Project, July 20, 1978. http://www.presidency.ucsb.edu/ws/?pid=31101.

Dworkin, Ronald. "Why Bakke Has No Case." *New York Review of Books*, November 10, 1977. http://www.nybooks.com/articles/1977/11/10/why-bakke-has-no-case.

Friedersdorf, Conor. "Does Affirmative Action Create Mismatches Between Students and Universities?" *Atlantic*, December 15, 2015. https://www.theatlantic.com/politics/archive/2015/12/the-needlessly-polarized-mismatch-theory-debate/420321.

Hall, Kermit J., Paul Finkelman, and James W. Ely Jr. *American Legal History: Cases and Materials*. 5th ed. New York: Oxford University Press, 2017.

Herman, Marc. "No One Tell Justice Thomas: Affirmative Action 'Mismatch Theory' Debunked Again." *Pacific Standard*, June 26, 2013. https://psmag.com/news/affirmative-action-mismatch-theory-debunked-again-no-one-tell-justice-thomas-61276.

Lauter, David. "Civil Rights Bill Vetoes by Bush." *Los Angeles Times*, October 23, 1990. http://articles.latimes.com/1990-10-23/news/mn-2961_1_civil-rights-leaders.

McBride, Alex. "Grutter v. Bollinger and Gratz v. Bollinger (2003)." PBS: The Supreme Court, December 2006. https://www.pbs.org/wnet/supremecourt/future/landmark_grutter.html.

Mintz, Morton. "The Bakke Case Decision." *Washington Post*, June 29, 1978. https://www.washingtonpost.com/archive/politics/1978/06/29/the-bakke-case-decision/0d91e8db-a171-4748-a731-16a248a4ad12/?utm_term=.ac683a09a6cc.

—. "Regents of University of California v. Bakke (1978)," PBS: The Supreme Court, December 2006. https://www.pbs.org/wnet/supremecourt/rights/landmark_regents.html.

Richter, Paul. "Clinton Declares Affirmative Action Is 'Good For America.'" *Los Angeles Times*, July 20, 1995. http://articles.latimes.com/1995-07-20/news/mn-26049_1_affirmative-action-programs.

Savage, Charlie. "Justice Department to Take On Affirmative Action in College Admissions." *New York Times*, August 1, 2017. https://www.nytimes.com/2017/08/01/us/politics/trump-affirmative-action-universities.html?_r=0.

"Split Ruling on Affirmative Action." NPR, June 23, 2003. http://www.npr.org/news/specials/michigan.

Weaver, Warren, Jr. "Justices Hear Bakke Arguments But Give Little Hint on Decision." *New York Times*, October 13, 1977. https://timesmachine.nytimes.com/timesmachine/1977/10/13/75688830.ml?action=click&login=smartlock&pageNumber=1.

Index

About the Author

Zachary Deibel is a social studies instructor at Cristo Rey Columbus High School in Columbus, Ohio. He holds a BA in history from American University and an MA in history from Arkansas State University. He enjoys reading, writing, and thinking about American history, government, and society with his students.

Affirmative Action
Regents of the University of California v. Bakke

Freedom of the Press
Crown v. John Peter Zenger

Interracial Marriage
Loving v. Virginia

Racial Segregation
Plessy v. Ferguson

Same-Sex Marriage
Obergefell v. Hodges

School Desegregation
Brown v. Board of Education of Topeka

Slavery and Citizenship
Dred Scott v. Sandford

Cavendish
Square

ISBN-13: 978-1502635822

9 781502 635822